W9-BSB-840

Weiss Ratings' Consumer Guide to Elder Care Choices

Weiss Ratings' Consumer Guide to Elder Care Choices

Spring 2020

GREY HOUSE PUBLISHING

Weiss Ratings
4400 Northcorp Parkway
Palm Beach Gardens, FL 33410
561-627-3300

Copyright © Weiss Ratings corporate headquarters located at 4400 Northcorp Parkway, Palm Beach Gardens, FL, 33410; telephone 561-627-3300. All rights reserved. This publication contains original and creative work and is fully protected by all applicable copyright laws, as well as by laws covering misappropriation, trade secrets and unfair competition. Additionally, Weiss Ratings has added value to the underlying factual material through one or more of the following efforts: unique and original selection; expression; arrangement; coordination; and classification. None of the content of this publication may be reproduced, stored in a retrieval system, redistributed, or transmitted in any form or by any means (electronic, print, mechanical, photocopying, recording or otherwise) without the prior written permission of Weiss Ratings. "Weiss Ratings" is a trademark protected by all applicable common law and statutory laws.

Independent. Unbiased. Accurate. Trusted.

Published by Grey House Publishing, Inc., located at 4919 Route 22, Amenia, NY 12501; telephone 518-789-8700. Grey House Publishing neither guarantees the accuracy of the data contained herein nor assumes any responsibility for errors, omissions or discrepancies. Grey House Publishing accepts no payment for listing; inclusion in the publication of any organization, agency, institution, publication, service or individual does not imply endorsement of the publisher.

4919 Route 22
PO Box 56
Amenia, NY 12501-0056

Spring 2020 Edition

ISBN: 978-1-64265-579-7
ISSN: 2165-395X

CONTENTS

Terms and Conditions

This document is prepared strictly for the confidential use of our customer(s). It has been provided to you at your specific request. It is not directed to, or intended for distribution to or use by, any person or entity who is a citizen or resident of or located in any locality, state, country or other jurisdiction where such distribution, publication, availability or use would be contrary to law or regulation or which would subject Weiss Ratings, LLC or its affiliates to any registration or licensing requirement within such jurisdiction.

No part of the analysts' compensation was, is, or will be, directly or indirectly, related to the specific recommendations or views expressed in this research report.

This document is not intended for the direct or indirect solicitation of business. Weiss Ratings, LLC, and its affiliates disclaim any and all liability to any person or entity for any loss or damage caused, in whole or in part, by any error (negligent or otherwise) or other circumstances involved in, resulting from or relating to the procurement, compilation, analysis, interpretation, editing, transcribing, publishing and/or dissemination or transmittal of any information contained herein.

Weiss Ratings, LLC has not taken any steps to ensure that the securities or investment vehicle referred to in this report are suitable for any particular investor. The investment or services contained or referred to in this report may not be suitable for you and it is recommended that you consult an independent investment advisor if you are in doubt about such investments or investment services. Nothing in this report constitutes investment, legal, accounting or tax advice or a representation that any investment or strategy is suitable or appropriate to your individual circumstances or otherwise constitutes a personal recommendation to you.

The ratings and other opinions contained in this document must be construed solely as statements of opinion from Weiss Ratings, LLC, and not statements of fact. Each rating or opinion must be weighed solely as a factor in your choice of an institution and should not be construed as a recommendation to buy, sell or otherwise act with respect to the particular product or company involved.

Past performance should not be taken as an indication or guarantee of future performance, and no representation or warranty, expressed or implied, is made regarding future performance. Information, opinions and estimates contained in this report reflect a judgment at its original date of publication and are subject to change without notice. Weiss Ratings, LLC offers a notification service for rating changes on companies you specify. For more information visit WeissRatings.com or call 1-877-934-7778. The price, value and income from any of the securities or financial instruments mentioned in this report can fall as well as rise.

This document and the information contained herein is copyrighted by Weiss Ratings, LLC. Any copying, displaying, selling, distributing or otherwise delivering of this information or any part of this document to any other person or entity is prohibited without the express written consent of Weiss Ratings, LLC, with the exception of a reviewer or editor who may quote brief passages in connection with a review or a news story.

Weiss Ratings' Mission Statement

Weiss Ratings' mission is to empower consumers, professionals, and institutions with high quality advisory information for selecting or monitoring a financial services company or financial investment. In doing so, Weiss Ratings will adhere to the highest ethical standards by maintaining our independent, unbiased outlook and approach to advising our customers.

Introduction

When it comes to our future we dream about the golden years as a time to relax and enjoy the fruits of many years of work, an endless vacation of traveling, visiting family and friends, and enjoying favorite hobbies. However, that dream could be difficult to achieve, unless you plan very carefully.

According to the Genworth Cost of Care Survey 2019 https://www.genworth.com/aging-and-you/finances/cost-of-care.html, among people turning 65 today, 70 percent will require some type of long-term care either in the community or at a facility. Furthermore, the average lifetime nursing home use per person is one year.[1] The bad news is that the national average cost for a private room and private paying patients was $280 per day in 2019. That's $102,200 a year! [1] If you have a family member living nearby ... or enough money to hire someone to help you with daily tasks ... or best of all, a combination of both, the probability of you needing a nursing home is reduced. But the time has come to go beyond just hoping. You need to put together a clear plan which includes:

a. a careful review of the lifestyle options that are going to be available,
b. a more precise vision of how you want to live when age starts slowing you down,
c. a reasonable estimate of how much money it's probably going to cost.

Fortunately, there are many options available:

There are continuing care communities that provide assisted living, if and when you need it. You can move in while you are still fully active. If you never need special assistance, fine. If you do need it, you can make arrangements almost immediately, and you won't have to move to a new place.

There are many ways to get care at home. If you really want to stay in your own home as you age, there are many home health services available. Registered nurses can administer medication. Home health aids can assist with bathing and other activities of daily living (ADLs). And if you have family nearby, they can help with household chores and daily errands.

---

[1] Source: Genworth June 2019

Your family members or primary caregivers can get help, too. This is especially important if you develop a debilitating illness, such as rheumatoid arthritis or Alzheimer's. Would they be able to handle the entire burden? If you yourself have cared for an ailing relative, you already know how stressful it can be, especially with all the other demands of today's world.

The True Impact of Long Term Care on Family Caregivers [3]

- 33 % spent more than 30 hours per week on care giving
- 66 % experienced care-related distractions such as phone calls and emails while working
- 60 % said care giving duties had negative effect on their jobs
- 46 % of caregivers spent more than $5,000 each year in care giving costs

To help reduce that stress for your loved ones, part of your planning should include finding out more about local organizations that will give your family members support. For example, if they have to work full-time, there are many senior daycare centers that provide meals and social activities, typically from 8 am to 5 pm each day.

Years ago, the choice was either nursing home or no nursing home. Now, as you can see, there are all kinds of different options available, which is great. The problem is deciding exactly how to fit the whole puzzle together is getting more and more complicated. That's where professional Care Managers can help. They specialize in helping you and your family figure out precisely which long-term care arrangements are best for you. They are experts on virtually all of the various options in your community. They know the costs, the benefits, the pros and the cons. They know the ins and outs of Medicare and health insurance eligibility and benefits. Just having someone to help with all the Medicare or Medicaid paperwork and red tape can be a huge relief for you.

However, I'm sure you don't want a Care Manager - no matter how qualified - to make your life decisions for you. So you will still need to gain as much knowledge about long-term care as you can. And the best time to do that is right now, *before* the time comes when you're under pressure to start actually making critical choices. This guide is designed to educate you and your loved ones on the many choices available and to provide you with the tools necessary to make an informed decision on living arrangements during your Golden Years.

---

[3] Source: Genworth May 2016

Getting Started

This guide will walk you through the steps of:

- Learning the kinds of facilities that are available to you and what they can offer
- Determining the pros and cons of each type of facility
- Getting a general idea of what you can expect to pay for each choice
- Finding the facilities in your area
- Putting together a list of questions for each facility you're interested in
- Contacting organizations that can give you specific information for individual facilities

First, review the types of facilities. You have five choices:

- Continuing Care Retirement Community
- Assisted Living Facility
- Home Health Care Agencies
- Adult Day Services
- Nursing Home

The chart below gives you a quick summary of what each type of facility provides, but read on for the full details since not all of these will fit your needs.

	Meals	House-keeping	Bathing	Dressing	Eating	Admin. of Med.	Trans-portation	Social Activities	24 Hour Assistance	Skilled Nursing Care
Assisted Living	X	X	X	X	X		X	X		
Home Health Care*	X	X	X	X	X	X				
Adult Day Services	X							X		
Respite Care	X		X	X	X	X			X	X
Nursing Home	X	X	X	X	X	X				X

*Services provided may not be available from some caregivers.

Continuing Care Retirement Community

If you're an active senior and you don't like change, this is ideal. Continuing Care Retirement Communities (CCRCs) also known as Life Care Communities, offer residences for all levels of need - with great flexibility to move from one to the other. So if your capabilities diminish as you age, you can shift to an assisted living area of the same community, without changing your lifestyle or having to make new friends. Plus, there's usually a wide range in what they offer - all the way from residences for fully independent seniors to facilities offering 24-hour care.

They're not cheap. But at least you know ahead of time what each facility will cost. For the most part, each level of residence has clear, established rates so you can review them ahead of time and plan your finances accordingly. You also get easy access to convenient health care, plus free usage of community facilities such as pool, fitness room and sauna. Plus, they offer one key advantage that many seniors find to be more difficult nowadays in their own communities - companionship of friends and neighbors of similar ages.

Here are the primary pros and cons:

Continuing Care Retirement Communities	
Pros:	*Cons:*
• Versatility	• Expensive
• Security	○ One-time entrance fee ranging from $100,000 to $750,000 or higher
• Access to health care	
• Community pool, fitness room, etc.	○ Fees of $2,500 to $10,700 per month[4]
• Companionship of peers	

The cost for these communities includes a one-time entrance fee along with monthly payments thereafter. Entrance fees range anywhere from $100,000 to $750,000 or higher. After that, fees range from $2,500 to $10,700 per month. Some CCRCs are affiliated with a specific religious or ethnic group and require membership along with the entrance fee.

---

[4] GAO (Government Accountability Office), June 2010

When you pay the entrance fee, they'll ask you to sign a contract which spells out the additional fees you're going to have to pay. Your contract can be one of the following three most common types:

- **Extensive contract.** You'll be entitled to unlimited long-term nursing care at little or no increase in the monthly fee.
- **Modified contract.** You'll get a specified amount of long-term nursing care. But then, after you exhaust that benefit, you'll be responsible for any additional payments.
- **Fee-for-service contract.** You pay as you go - the daily rates are based on the number of services they provide you.

Only you can decide which contract is best for you. Naturally, the extensive contract is going to be the most expensive up front; the fee-for-service contract, the least expensive up front. If you're concerned about your present or future health, you want peace of mind, and you can afford it, then favor the extensive contract. If you're confident in your health or you can't afford it, then favor one of the other two options.

Important: Some Continuing Care Retirement Communities may require applicants to have Medicare Part A and B and/or an exam to assess mental and physical status.

How to Find the Continuing Care Retirement Community That's Best for You

The first place to check is the Commission on Accreditation of Rehabilitation Facilities which acquired the Continuing Care Accreditation Commission (CARF-CCAC), the only accrediting body for continuing care facilities. The CARF-CCAC maintains the list of standards a community must meet in order to be accredited. Plus, it has a list of all the facilities that are currently accredited.

CARF-CCAC uses a set of standards called ASPIRE to Excellence® that assesses quality from three perspectives - organizational structure, processes, and outcomes. The framework has six basic categories:

- **A**ssess the environment
- **S**et Strategy
- **P**ersons-served & Other Stakeholders - Obtain input
- **I**mplement the plan
- **R**eview results
- **E**ffect Change

If you want more information on the ASPIRE to Excellence standards call CARF-CCAC toll-free at (866) 888-1122 or go to www.carf.org.

Needless to say, setting standards is one thing. Enforcing those standards in every facility, every day of the year, is another. But now, when you visit a community, you can know what to look for. Use their standards as your checklist, especially if you happen to be interested in a community which is not yet accredited.

www.carf.org is the place to start shopping for accredited communities. If you want to contact the CARF-CCAC, go to their website. Address and phone numbers are listed, as well as, an email inquiry form you can fill out and send.

Assisted Living Facility

No one looks forward to the day they may lose their independence. But we all know the day is bound to come sooner or later. Despite all our efforts, we'll be too strained or exhausted to complete all daily activities on our own. When that happens to us, we definitely don't want to be without the help we'll need.

Even if a Continuing Care Retirement Community is your first choice, for comparison purposes, you may also want to look into Assisted Living Facilities. In these kinds of facilities, you can still be relatively independent, but the worry and stress of performing certain daily tasks can be mostly removed. These facilities have all kinds of titles and names, such as:

- Residential care
- Personal care
- Adult congregate living care
- Board and care
- Domiciliary care
- Adult living facilities
- Supported care

- Enhanced care
- Community-based retirement facilities
- Adult foster care
- Adult homes
- Sheltered housing
- Retirement residences

But don't let the different names fool you. They're all basically Assisted Living Facilities. Typically, the services they give you include assistance with meals, medications, bathing, dressing, laundry, shopping and transportation.The place could be a high rise or single story. They may have one- or two-bedroom units or double-occupancy rooms, more or less like a hotel. Naturally, costs will be all over the lot, depending upon the amenities, the room size, and the geographic location, but the national average, private pay monthly rate is $4,051 or $48,612 per year. [5]

---

[5] Genworth June 2019

But remember: These facilities are not nursing homes. They are not intended for around-the-clock nursing. Instead, they cater to seniors who are more or less independent and just need occasional assistance with certain tasks.

Typically, when you're being admitted to an Assisted Living Facility, they'll evaluate the level of care you need. Then, about one month later, they'll do a second evaluation to get a more precise idea of what level of assistance you need. From that point forward, they'll do periodic re-assessments if you, the staff, or your family think it's necessary or if your health status changes. Ultimately, if your health deteriorates beyond the abilities of the facility, you may have to move to a nursing home.

However, Assisted Living Facilities have several clear advantages:

- They let you keep your independence without the strain of daily chores.
- Double check yourself, but as a rule, it should cost you less than some of your other options, such as staying at home with professional daily assistance.
- You'll have friends and social activities right there. That's probably going to be a lot more convenient than traveling or moving around to see friends. If you stay at home and you or your friends can't or don't want to drive around or take transportation, you'll start losing touch with each other, becoming more isolated, fixated on TV or talking mostly on the phone. Don't let that happen to you.

The main disadvantage of an Assisted Living Facility is the *limit* to the kind of assistance they can give you. Assisted living is just that - living on your own with support for a few tasks. It is **not** an alternative to a nursing home. That's why many facilities will not accept residents who need respirators or catheters. If you find yourself in this situation, a nursing home is usually the best alternative.

If you're in relatively good health and can handle the majority of day-to-day living, with the exception of a few tasks, then an Assisted Living Facility is a good option to consider.

They usually deliver meals three times a day with housekeeping and laundry done on a scheduled basis. The care providers may *remind* you when to take medications, but they're usually not allowed to actually administer the medications, due to state regulations. For that, you'd need a nurse.

Many facilities also have a separate program catering to Alzheimer's patients or those with mild dementia. But those areas are often separated from the other areas and kept secure at all times to prevent a resident from wandering away.

Before going on to the rest of the discussion about assisted living facilities, there's one truly critical issue you need to think about:

Who's The Boss?

Let's say you have some difficulty walking. And let's say that you refuse to be tied down to a walker - let alone a wheelchair. Your position is: "Give me my cane and leave me alone, thank you very much. It's my life and my risk to take."

Now ask yourself: Do you want to be living in a place that backs off and lets you assume that responsibility for yourself? Or would you prefer a place where you're essentially *required* to follow their standards, for your own safety. If you're stubbornly independent like most people, your natural tendency will be to favor the former. But think about it. It's not a black-or-white decision. A bad fall causing a broken bone, like a hip, can often turn out to be the beginning of a long demise. You certainly want to do everything you can to avoid that fate.

Yes, the main reason you'd choose an assisted living facility in the first place is precisely because of the independence they offer. You don't want someone to be continually telling you what to do, what and when to eat, and how you move about. But there's a limit. You may actually *want* someone to at least *remind* you not to do things that may hurt you.

You may even want someone to *prevent* you from doing those things, like a strong guard rail on a dangerous mountain road.

No matter what, make sure you seriously consider this aspect when choosing a facility, and continue to consider it periodically after being admitted to a facility. Many facilities boast the "dignity of risk," meaning that you can keep your dignity and make your own decision, even if those decisions jeopardize your safety. This gives you a greater sense of control. Others may not give you that freedom. Many even require that you sign a contract outlining how much risk you are allowed to take versus how much risk the facility will take. This is okay, but be sure to read the contract carefully. This alone could make the difference between a life full of satisfaction versus a life full of daily aggravations.

Assisted Living Facilities

Pros:
- Independence retained
- Assistance with meals, medications, bathing, dressing, laundry, shopping, and transportation
- Companionship of peers
- Less expensive than a CCRC

Cons:
- Limits to levels of assistance
- Will not accept residents with respirators or catheters

Again, as with the Continuing Care Retirement Communities, cost for theses facilities vary all over the lot. You pay more for a better location, bigger rooms, superior amenities, and top-notch service. You pay less for cheaper locations, smaller rooms, less-than-ideal amenities and not-so-great service.

But there's another important financial consideration. You or your family usually has to foot almost the entire bill. Yes, Medicaid may pay for a small portion of facilities. But as a rule, financing is private.

What about long-term care insurance? Yes, many policies do cover Assisted Living Facilities, but check each policy first to make sure exactly what *their* exact definition of Assisted Living is. It may or may not include the facility you are looking at. For more information on long-term care insurance, see Weiss Ratings' *Consumer Guide to Long-Term Care Insurance* (available at www.financialratingsseries.com/page/pr_boxset).

What You Should Look for in an Assisted Living Facility

Next step, visit some facilities. When you do, here are some tips on what to look for:

1. The very first thing you'll probably be looking at is the facility's cleanliness and aesthetics. Is it well kept? Is the décor pleasing? But also check to make sure it has:

   - Handrails in the hallways and bathrooms that you can grasp easily

   - Ways you can call for help whenever you need it

   - Good lighting

   - Easily accessible cabinets and closets

   - Exits that are well marked in case of emergencies

   - Also no trivial matter: Simple carpeting and wall color. Reason: busy patterns can make it difficult to see in a hallway

Warning: Staff or family members may focus too much on the décor and superficial appearances. That's all fine and dandy. But provided the facility is well kept and clean, you know darn well that safety and practicality are more important. So make sure they know that's your priority.

2. Also observe the staff and their interaction with residents. Are staff members open and friendly? Are the residents in the main areas of the facility, or are most of them in their rooms, alone? Since one of the purposes of an Assisted Living Facility is social interaction, facilities should encourage communication among residents. A friendly staff is very important, but the best measure of a facility is its residents.

   - Do they appear happy and outgoing?

   - Does the staff relate to the residents?

   - Do they use their names when speaking?

   - Do they seem genuinely interested in the residents?

Warning: If they say the facility is "half full" (which really means "half empty," or worse), watch out. Unless it's a brand new facility just beginning to attract residents, it could indicate financial troubles on the horizon.

3. The tour is over and the facility has passed all your initial screens. Now, it's time to sit down and start asking some tough, detailed questions, such as:

    • **What types of services are available?** Here are the standard services offered at virtually all good facilities:

        o   three meals a day

        o   housekeeping

        o   laundry

        o   transportation

        o   assistance with activities of daily living (ADLs)

        o   access to medical services

        o   health and exercise programs

        o   medication management

        o   social and recreational activities

    These are the bare-bones basics. So if you find that one or more of these common services is *not* offered by the facility as part of its services, something's probably wrong. Seriously consider scratching the place off your list. How and how much they charge for each of these can vary. For example, some may offer all meals and laundry for just one package fee. Others many charge separately. That's not a problem, as long as the services *are* available.

Warning: If they tell you the facility has "access to medical services," be aware that this does *not* mean that you can receive long-term nursing care while living in the facility. It means that if you should have an accident or unexpected health problem, the facility will provide immediate care for *that* event only - not long-term rehabilitation or ongoing care.

- **Exactly what is included in the daily/monthly rate?** When you check into a hotel for a night, it's not going to ruin you if you find out later that they've charged you $1 for each local call. But when you move into an Assisted Living Facility for the next few years, imagine getting charged $50 every time you need off-hours transportation to the nearest store! Make sure you have a very clear idea of *how often* you have access to the standard benefits included in your daily or monthly rate. Can you be transported at any time or are there limitations? Can you get housekeeping services *whenever* you wish? Are social and recreational activities included? Make sure they tell you exactly what they give you as part of the standard rate versus what costs extra.

- **What extra services are available and for what fee?** Suppose you want some special service that is not part of its standard choices - maybe Internet access or a special diet. Could the facility provide the service? If so, how much would it cost? You should find out how much it charges for *all* of the services you consider essential.

- **Are services provided by the facility's employees, or are arrangements made with other agencies?** You would prefer to have the facility's employees performing the services so that 1) you are familiar with the care providers; 2) the care providers are familiar with your situation and needs; and 3) the facility has more control over the caregivers. If too many essential services are provided by outside companies, it could be a drawback.

- **What are the choices for accommodations?** There is no standard on this one. Many of the facilities offer a private living area with a common area for meals and social activities. The structure is generally a two- to three-story apartment-style building, with one to two bedroom units. All units should have a private bath, and some will even include a full kitchen or kitchenette.

Important: Some facilities may force you to share your room with one or more residents, which is something you probably don't want to do. Be sure to find out if this is the case or if you have your own room.

Equally important: Be sure to actually *see* the accommodations before you make a commitment.

- **What kinds of recreational activities are available?** Are the activities and outside trips geared toward the individual or are they group oriented? Having the freedom to take advantage of facilities individually is OK, but if the facility is not giving you the opportunity to interact with other residents through group recreational activities, you will be missing out on one of the main advantages of an Assisted Living Facility.

- **How much control will you have over your schedule?** You want to be the one who decides when you eat, when you bath, when you go to the store, or when you need laundry done. Will you be able to do that or will your schedule be dictated by when others say you have to do those things?

- **Do you get to choose when to get help and how often?** Be sure to ask how you go about accessing the services provided. Ideally you want to be able to call at any time to request services, but that may not be realistic. Find out if (a) you can just sign up on a schedule for the services, as you need them, or (b) there are limited, predetermined times that you must adhere to. Try to find what works best for you and would cause the least disruption to what you're used to.

- **How does the facility assess the level of care that is needed and how often is the situation reassessed?** Your needs can change quickly so you want your situation reassessed relatively often, say once every few months, or as needed if you become unexpectedly impaired.

4. Don't forget to address special needs and find out what the facility's plan of care is. This is also the time to discuss the whole issue of supervision vs. autonomy which was discussed earlier. How much input do you and your family have with regard to your care? If the staff personnel are the only ones who can decide which of your needs are to be met and when, scratch this place off your list too, and move on.

5. Be wary of the term "negotiated risk." Yes, it supports consumer choice and independence. But also may be a clever way for facilities to avoid liability. The more independence and autonomy for you, the consumer, the less liability that exists for the facility. Although you may be attracted to the idea that you have complete control over your life, the reality is that today you must protect your interests, just as the facility wants to protect its interests and avoid potential lawsuits.

Going back to the earlier example about the cane vs. the walker, suppose some careless janitors leave behind a wet, slippery floor with no warning signs. Shouldn't the facility be responsible for the consequences, both legally and ethically? They should not be allowed to use the excuse "we told you to use the walker, but you decided to use the cane."

Specifically, here are some guiding principles:

a. The more risk a facility assumes, the more incentive they have to keep the environment safe and clean.

b. The facility has the right to expect you to act in a safe manner, in order to prevent potential accidents.

c. A facility should recognize your desire for independence but not easily step away from the responsibility of risk.

All of these responsibilities and expectations of both you and the facility should be discussed before admission. Make sure it's all spelled out clearly and you're happy with the terms.

6. Happy with everything so far? Good. Now comes the final step: The contract, or the admission agreement. Don't sign it on the spot. Take it home with you. Review it carefully at your leisure. Remember, this is a lot more than a standard lease, and you need to scrutinize a lot more than just your tenancy and payment. The contract should also cover essential operational issues - precisely what the facility does and how it will get it done. If possible, have a lawyer review it, and make sure you understand everything. Unintelligible legalese can often hide serious issues that can return to haunt you later.

For more information on Assisted Living Facilities, you may contact the American Health Care Association and National Center for Assisted Living (NCAL) at their website www.careconversations.org or by calling (202) 842-4444.

You can also call LeadingAge at (202) 783-2242 or visit their website at www.leadingage.org.

Home Health Care

Aside from the comfort of living in their own home, older folks have a more specific reason for not wanting to move. As their facilities diminish, they learn to rely on familiarity and memory to move about. So moving into an unfamiliar residence can be extremely stressful and upsetting. That's why so many like staying put in their own home. It's certainly a viable choice. Home health care includes a wide array of services, including medical, nursing, social and therapeutic sessions, provided by the following types of businesses or organizations:

- Home health agencies
- Homemaker and home care aide agencies
- Staffing and private-duty agencies

- Pharmaceutical and infusion therapy companies
- Durable equipment and supply dealers
- Registries and hospice

How to Choose A Good Agency

All of the agencies usually make care available to you 24 hours a day, 7 days a week. All of them give you assistance individually or as a team. Some may charge on an hourly or daily basis, depending upon your needs. Some may give you mostly one-stop shopping - offering a variety of *different* services, including assistance with meals, bathing, dressing and housekeeping. Some may be more specialized, offering just one or two of these services. But none of these issues distinguish the good from the bad. Instead, be sure to ask these questions:

1. Are you licensed by the state? In most states they have to be licensed to meet minimum standards. But in some states they are not licensed. Be sure to ask anyhow.
2. Are you Medicare certified? If they are, they meet federal standards required to administer care to Medicare or Medicaid patients. If they're not certified, you shouldn't be doing business with this agency.

Can You Hire Your Own Home Care Providers Without An Agency?

Most home care aide agencies recruit and supervise their own personnel and are therefore liable for the care rendered. Other agencies, also liable for the care rendered, include private-duty agencies, pharmaceutical and infusion therapy companies, durable medical equipment and supply dealers, and hospices. Plus, there are registries that act as employment agencies for home care nurses and aides.

Can you just bypass all these agencies and hire your own helpers yourself, directly? Sure. There are usually plenty of nurses, therapists and aides, chore workers and companions available for hire. And you may save some money.

Two drawbacks:

- They may not be licensed or meet specified government standards.
- If they get sick or don't show up for work for some reason, you're the one who has to scramble to find a replacement.

There are several advantages to staying at home:

- Your surroundings remain unchanged.
- You can continue with your regular daily routine (especially important if you have waning eyesight and rely on the familiarity of your home).
- A sudden change in surroundings can lead to insecurity and emotional stress, which in turn can even lead to illness and depression for some people.
- You save the money of moving expenses.

But there are also critical disadvantages:

- You may not have the support of a social network.

- You may wind up being relatively isolated.

- If you are unable to drive, or shouldn't be driving due to poor eyesight or diminishing mental state, it may become more difficult to attend social events.

Home Health Care	

Pros:
• Stay in your own home
• Often more affordable than care in a facility
• Many services available 24 hours a day, 7 days a week
   o Medical but varies widely
   o Nursing
   o Social
   o Therapeutic
	Cons:
	• Feelings of isolation may be experienced if unable to leave home
	• National average hourly rate for home health aides is $23[6]

A Broad Array of Caregivers

There's a clear pecking order of caregivers, each trained and licensed to give you a different level of care:

- **Registered Nurses (RNs)** must have at least two years of training and be licensed by the state. They offer the highest level of care and are typically the most expensive.

- **Licensed Practice Nurses (LPNs)** usually have at least one year of training and are supervised by RNs.

- **Certified Nurse Assistants (CNAs)** also must have a minimum number of training hours and are generally supervised by RNs.

---

[6] Genworth June 2019

- **Home Health Aids** provide assistance with the activities of daily living (ADLs) but are not medically trained.
- **Personal Assistants or Attendants** are similar to home health aids but cater mostly to people with disabilities.
- **Homemakers** help with light housekeeping duties but do not provide personal care.

Plus: **Private Geriatric Care Managers** help with decision making related to the level and location of care, recommending homecare as appropriate.

At first, home care may appear to be one of the least expensive options. But be careful. You might calculate your costs thinking that all you need is a homemaker and an occasional personal attendant only to discover that what you really need is a home health aid and an occasional RN. And there's a huge difference in the costs. So try to map out, as best you can, the actual level of care you think you will be needing, and don't forget to factor in the costs of the actual professionals you will be using.

Some people also overspend. They may hire a full-time RN when all they really need is a home health aid with an RN available to come and visit once a week or once a month.

Be sure to compare home care cost to nursing homes in your area. Nationwide there is only a small difference in the average daily cost of having a home health aide at $144, and a homemaker at $141. However, if you also need visits from a RN , your total daily cost may actually be more than the average daily rate for a private room at a nursing home, which is currently $280 per day.[7]

---

[7] Genworth June 2019

Here are the average costs of nursing homes.

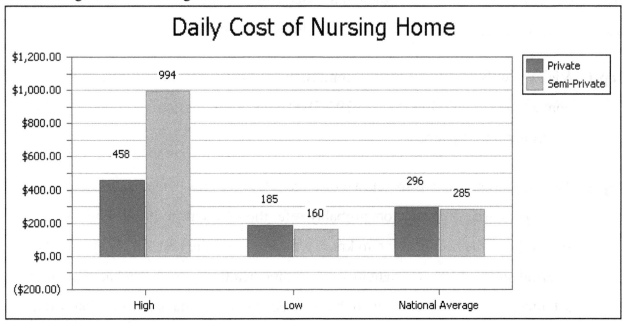

Source: Genworth

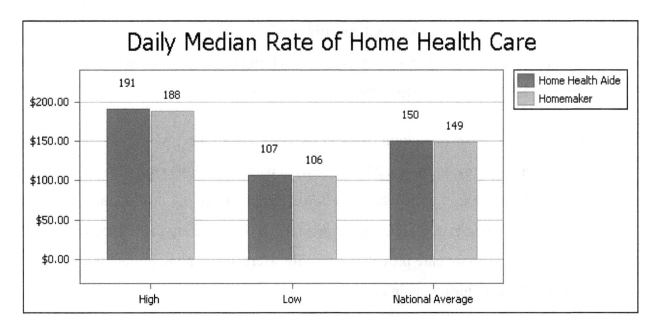

Source: Genworth

How To Find The Right Home Health Care Agency For You

No two agencies are created equal. Although all Medicare-certified facilities do meet minimum standards, some do a much better job than others. Follow these steps:

Step 1 Visit the website of The Joint Commission at www.jointcommission.org. Or, you can contact the commission at (630) 792-5800. Joint Commission has a home health care accreditation program.

Step 2 Talk to your physicians to get two or three references for home health care services that cover your area. Your doctors probably refer their patients to these services all the time and should be in the best position to know which ones do the best job. They usually have no ax to grind and will tell you right away if a home health agency has a bad reputation. Always ask more than one doctor though, because each one may have a somewhat different set of experiences to share with you. As with any second opinion, if more than one doctor agrees, you know you're on the right track.

Step 3 Call the agencies to find out what specific services they provide (e.g., assistance with bathing, toileting, dressing, cooking). But don't rely on the phone alone. If the agency provides the services you need, then move on to the next step.

Step 4 Always make *at least one* initial visit to the company to meet with some of the caregivers before reaching any decisions. Many agencies will say: "Don't worry about coming to our offices. We'll come to you." That may be very convenient, but it does not serve your purpose of finding the best agency. Remember: You are hiring them - not vice-versa. So interview your future care providers carefully. Here are some important questions you should ask them during the interview:

- How long have you been in business? Avoid companies that are just starting out, even if the staff has plenty of experience with other companies.

- What local references can you give me? They should be able to give you several.

- How much do you charge for each service? Make sure you compare these charges to at least one or two other agencies.

- What is your screening process for hiring caregivers?

- Do you have a specific training program for your newly hired caregivers? Tell me about it.

- How do you supervise your caregivers?

- I assume you will let me and my family be involved in our plan of care. How does that work?

- Will I always, or almost always, get the same caregiver for the same service? Or will they rotate all the time? Usually, they should assign just *one* person for each service, plus one back-up. For example, if you've had an injury, you should always get the same physical therapist, unless the therapist is sick or on vacation.

- What happens in an emergency

These questions should be answered easily and directly. Local references should be offered, along with literature explaining the company's services, eligibility requirements, fees, and a detailed "Patient Bill of Rights" explaining the rights and responsibilities of all parties involved. The more information and education that is offered the better. Remember, you will be dealing with these people on a regular basis, so it's pertinent that you trust and feel comfortable with them.

Respite Care

If you're seriously ill and require 24-hour care by family or friends, respite care may be something *they* will need as much as you do. Everyone needs a break at times, and respite care offers a temporary break for your caregiver, so that your care will not become too stressful for him or her.

To be eligible for respite assistance, your caregiver must be at least 18 years old, unpaid and provide at least 16 hours of care a day. (That seems like a lot, but it's the standard).

Trained respite care providers offer assistance in or out of the home, hourly and 24-hour care, for planned and emergency situations. There are different levels of care, from companionship, supervision, and meal preparation to daily activities, such as dressing and bathing. Licensed nurses can also provide respite care if you have special medical care or require administration of medications.

Respite care is offered through hospice, local nursing registry organizations, and various home health organizations. Many of these organizations are non-profit, and base their pricing on the financial status of your caregiver. Hospice is one of the largest providers of respite care, and primarily operates as a not-for-profit entity, relying heavily on private donations.

Adult Day Services

There's probably no better way to reduce the cost of long-term care than by living with your family. You avoid those high entry tickets into Continuing Care Retirement Communities. You save on the high monthly costs of Assisted Living Facilities. You can even cut down dramatically on the home care costs.

What if your family members have to go to work every day, and you can't stay home alone? That's where Adult Day Services comes in.

Adult Day Services are also known as Adult Day Care Centers or Senior Centers. They are usually in your local community, often run by the community for seniors, including seniors that are functionally impaired or cognitively impaired. They offer structured, comprehensive day programs. They provide a variety of health, social, and other support services. And they generally do it all at a reasonable cost.

You get dropped off at the center in the morning. You participate in their programs throughout the day with the supervision of qualified professionals. And then you're picked up in the late afternoon. Meanwhile, your family members can go to work and take care of their business, helping to at least partially reduce the burden on them - along with any remorse you might have of "interfering with their lives." Remember: There's no such thing as a perfect solution.

Who can you expect to meet at an adult day care center? Well, the average age is 72, and about two out of three of the people there will probably be women. About one half will be very alert, while the other half could have some cognitive impairment. All told, it is estimated that there are over 4,000 adult day care centers in the United States today, with most operating on a nonprofit or public basis.[8]

---

[8] Adult Day Care http://www.adultdaycare.org/resources/who-uses-adult-day-care-/

Your cost? Daily fees will vary depending on the number of hours you attend the program, how much they get in outside funding, and what kinds of services they offer. Average cost across the country is approximately $72.[9]

The main drawbacks: There is a cost. Plus, if the center's schedule doesn't match up with the schedule of your family members, *someone* in the family is going to have to make *some* sacrifices. Although some people may feel that way, these places are *not* child care centers. They're for adults and they give you a safe environment, along with the companionship of peers. Most important, they give you the opportunity to continue living with your loved ones - in their home or yours.

Adult Day Services	
Pros:	*Cons:*
• Safe Environment	• Often compared to child day care
• Companionship of peers	• Limited hours of operation
• Accessible locations	• Additional cost

How to Find Good Adult Day Services

Follow these steps:

Step 1   Put together a short list of your basic needs based on the following questions:

- How much assistance do you need to perform daily activities, such as walking, eating, and toileting?
- Do you have any need for specialized physical or occupational therapies?
- What type of health *monitoring* do you need for specific conditions, such as diabetes?
- Do you have any special diet?
- What are the minimum hours you and your family need the center to be open?

---

[9] Genworth June 2018

Step 2 Next, put together a list of acceptable Adult Day Care Centers in your area. You can do that by:

- Calling 1-800-677-1116. They'll give you the name and number for the Area Agency on Aging nearest you. Then, the Area Agency will refer you to local Adult Day Care Centers.
  Go to Eldercare locator (www.eldercare.gov)

- Talk to your physicians. Again, they probably have many patients attending these centers and would know which ones are the best, especially in terms of how they handle medical emergencies and care.

- Check the yellow pages. Look under terms such as "Adult Day Services," "Aging Services," or "Senior Citizens' Services."

Step 3 From Steps 1 and 2, you should now have two lists - one list of your needs, and one of the centers in your area. Call each potential center and ask them if they can meet your needs. Make sure they send you a brochure or pamphlet to give you a clearer idea of what they have to offer. This way, you don't have to waste time visiting centers that don't even meet your basic requirements.

Step 4 Time to visit. Check them out and make sure they adhere to these basic guidelines:

- If they take virtually any and all comers without further ado, something's wrong from the outset. They should conduct a careful assessment of every individual before admitting them to determine their abilities and needs and whether the center can meet those needs.

- If they take a cookie-cutter approach and put everyone in exactly the same program, that's not good either. They should develop an individualized plan for each participant.

- If they can kick you out on a whim, it's a no go. They should have clear criteria and guidelines for the termination of service.

- They should provide a broad range of services, such as personal care, transportation, meals, counseling and rehabilitative services.

- Their staff and volunteers should be qualified and well-trained. You may not be able to tell from the first visit to the first center. But when you've seen three or four, you can begin to discern the differences.

- Needless to say, they've got to meet or exceed state standards and guidelines. Search online for "Adult Day Centers State Standards" to find the link to your states guidelines.

Remember, regardless of how impressed you may be with any one center that you visit, always make sure you check at least three or four. And again, as with the Assisted Living Facilities, don't be fooled by fancy. It's the quality of care you should be most concerned with.

Nursing Home

Nursing homes have a bad reputation, and let's face it, it's often a much deserved one. But you should keep an open mind about them. Indeed, over the past decade, quite a few nursing homes have upgraded the level of care they offer. They used to be a last resort for seniors with diminishing capabilities. Now though, many of them are beginning to look and feel more like hospitals, with the goal of rehabilitating patients and getting them back home as soon as possible.

Since there's so much new competition for nursing homes now - the retirement communities, the assisted living facilities, and the adult day centers - the nursing homes are focusing on patients in need of special therapies.

If you've had a stroke, you can go to a nursing home for speech therapy and physical therapy. They can provide specialty care for patients with Alzheimer's, cancer, dementia, neuromuscular diseases, pulmonary disease and wound care.

Some nursing facilities work in conjunction with home health care agencies, adult day care, and respite care. Nursing homes are certified by local and federal governments to provide levels of care that can only be delivered by trained professionals. They provide the highest level of skilled care of any type of eldercare facility.

Nursing Home	
Pros:	*Cons:*
• Highest level of care	• Expensive
• Accommodate special needs	• Transition can be difficult

Again, this level of care does not come cheap. Nursing homes can cost anywhere from $4,227 to $20,000 per month, depending upon the location, the level of care needed and amenities offered. Therefore, the sooner you can return to one of the other alternatives, the better.

How to Find the Nursing Home That's Right for You

If you are researching nursing homes, it's probably not by choice, but by necessity. Therefore, it's assumed you've already made the decision on whether or not a nursing home is needed - most likely with the help of your family, your doctor or your caregiver. It's not too late to review that decision, though. Check some of the other alternatives again. Before you make the leap, make sure you really do need a nursing home.

Once you're convinced that's the way to go, now your goal is to find the best nursing home suitable for you. Time for more research!

Step 1   As with the other facilities described so far, doctors and other healthcare professionals are among the best sources for references, especially if they are familiar with your personal needs. Family and friends may also have recommendations, based on their own experiences with loved ones. But be sure that your family members are including *you* in any discussions regarding your care, and make sure that they are aware of your personal wishes. Explain to them that your involvement is vital in order for you to maintain your self respect and dignity.

Step 2   Together, make a list of what criteria is required from a potential residence - therapies, amount of care, special dietary needs. Be sure to include any preferences you have. You and your family should then answer these questions:

- Do you need special therapy such as speech, occupational or physical therapy?
- Do you have special dietary needs - to control diabetes, for instance?
- How important is a private room to you? What about a semi-private room?
- How important is the location? (The more convenient the location is to family, the more opportunities there are for visits.)
- What about the affiliation such as religious or ethnic group? Is that an issue?

- Do you have any old friends or family who are already staying at a facility? If so, that can go a long way to combating loneliness!

Step 3 Don't overlook the details. Keep in mind that sometimes it's the little things, such as having a window to look out of, that can make a real difference. The more input you provide to your loved ones, the easier it will be to make a decision that you and your family will be happy with. The more satisfied you are entering the nursing home, the better chance you have of returning to a less intensive care and less costly facility, such as assisted living.

Step 4 Start your search without leaving home. You may have an ideal setting in mind, but you probably won't be able to find it in the immediate vicinity. Most likely you will want to find a place close to where you live, or where other family members live, and limit it to a 25-50 mile radius. Start with selecting a certain area, and then get a list of all the nursing homes within that radius. On the Internet, visit www.nursinghomeinfo.com. It will do most of the searching for you, based on your city and state. Plus, it will also select for you based on your needs, including special medical needs, desired activities, amenities, religious affiliation, and even your preferred language. If you do not have access to the Internet, find someone who does. It can be anyone - a child, a grandchild or even your financial planner or accountant.

Step 5 Now you should have a much shorter list of nursing homes in your area that meet all your basic needs. How do you know if they pass muster? Actually, there are several sources that can help you:

- Ombudsman programs can give you inspection results of the nursing homes you request. Every state is required to have such a program. To find your local office, just contact the national organization at www.ltcombudsman.org or at (202) 332-2275.

- HealthGrades.com will give an evaluation of the nursing home of your choice. For more information go to www.healthgrades.com.

- Medicare (www.medicare.gov or 1-800-MEDICARE) offers a free interactive tool that gives comparison information about nursing homes, such as number of beds, whether it is Medicare or Medicaid certified, resident characteristics, summary information about the last state inspection, and the number of people on staff, along with their licensing qualifications.

Step 6 Now you're ready for actual visits. For a complete rundown, use the Nursing Home Checklist provided in the Appendix. Plus, when you visit, be on the alert for the following:

- How is the interaction between residents and staff?

- Does the staff seem familiar with residents?

- Is the interaction mostly cold and business-like or friendly and warm?

- How is the general disposition of the residents? Are they alert? Do they address the staff by name?

- Is the atmosphere generally upbeat and friendly, in terms of both residents and staff?

Step 7 Once you have narrowed your list to a few choices, visit the homes a second time for an independent tour. Look for consistency between visits in regards to cleanliness, health of residents, and staff demeanor. Pay extra attention to the residents and staff. Regardless of how nice a facility appears, it's the staff that affects the residents the most, both physically and emotionally.

Step 8 Stay involved in the decision from the beginning to the end. We can't stress this enough. Make sure your family members read it too: The transition from a private community to a nursing home can be difficult. So always make your preferences known to your family members. Once you've narrowed your choices down to a few final candidates that provide essentially the same basic needs, your final choice should be based upon those things that will make you the happiest and the most comfortable. It could be because you'll be with friends or others with similar ethnic backgrounds or religious beliefs. It could be because it's a facility closest to your grandchildren. Whatever the case, if it's important to you, it should be important to your family too.

Care Managers

If you do need hospice or 24-hour care, but feel insecure about handling the day-to-day issues that arise without the recommendation of a trusted confidant, then you may want to consider the services of a Care Manager. An Elder Care Manager (also known as a Geriatric Care Manager) helps you and your family make informed decisions about long-term care arrangements and other difficult decisions.

Their training is usually in gerontology, social work, nursing, or counseling. Many work independently, while others work for an established agency with three or more Care Managers together. Some agencies have experts in several areas, such as health, social work, accounting and legal professions, in order to handle the various issues that you might confront today. Other agencies employ Care Managers with well-rounded backgrounds, so their clients only have to deal with one person.

Geriatric Care Managers assist you in a wide variety of areas. They can assess the level of care needed, identify problems and find out if you are eligible for different types of assistance. They can also help arrange, screen and supervise in-home services. An important quality of a Care Manager is experience with the financial and legal issues directly related to the elderly. Certain Care Managers may specialize in financial or legal matters, and although your care manager may not be an expert, he should know someone who is.

Care Managers are especially beneficial should you not have family living close by. You may be able to function on a daily basis with little trouble, even performing tasks such as laundry and cooking very well.

However, a Care Manager is most beneficial when problems arise and a family member is not there to assess the situation first hand. The Care Manager is able to assess your needs, determine if additional assistance is necessary, make doctor's appointments and arrange transportation to those appointments. Care Managers also help with unplanned occurrences, such as broken appliances, house repairs and other problems. Knowing that there is someone looking out for you, even if your family is not nearby, can be a great comfort.

A Geriatric Care Manager can assess your needs in finding a suitable retirement home should the situation become necessary. Some Geriatric Care Managers also provide family therapy, money management, and guardianship assistance. They usually have extensive knowledge about the costs, quality and availability of services in the community. One of the most important roles of a care manager is the unbiased opinion they offer regarding the level of care you need. Making a decision about the level of care you need, especially if you don't want to admit what your true needs are, can be very difficult. It is also difficult for your family members. A Care Manager takes the burden off you and the guilt off your family if a higher level of care becomes necessary.

When looking for a Geriatric Care Manager, focus on credentials and experience. At minimum, a GCM should hold a clinical or graduate degree in social work, nursing, or psychology. Experience is important, but reputation in the community can also tell you a lot. A good Care Manager should be open and out-going, easy with rapport. He or she should also be results-oriented; specific on how, what, where and when. Remember, you are hiring the person for assessment and decision-making skills first and foremost. The following is a list of important questions you should ask a potential Care Manager:

- How long have you been in business?
- What licenses do you hold that allow independent practice?
- How do you handle crises? Are you available 24 hours?
- Who do you utilize for backup? What credentials or qualifications do you hold?
- What are your fees and exactly what services do you provide?

As with any interview, look for precise and direct answers, not flowery explanations. If it is a business that uses several care managers, get all their qualifications and experience. If there is a certain area that you need help in, for instance financial management, choose an agency that has a CPA. If you desire one-on-one assistance, look at smaller agencies that may offer more personalized service.

Costs for a Geriatric Care Manager vary depending on the level of expertise and the number of services expected. However, the benefits of personalized services, accessibility and continuity of care may well be worth it. If you are interested in finding a Aging Life Care expert in your area, you can contact the Aging Life Care Association at (520) 881-8008 for a local chapter or visit their website at www.aginglifecare.org.

Now that you're aware of the vast array of eldercare choices available, begin to make a game plan. Talk with your spouse about your wishes for the future. Talk to your family. Be clear in your desires for your future care.

If you would like to relocate to a certain Assisted Living Facility or CCRC, contact them and find out potential costs and if there's a waiting list. With the ever increasing senior population, many facilities have waiting lists of five years or more.

If you haven't already, you may want to consider long-term care insurance. You can learn more from Weiss Ratings' *Consumer's Guide to Long-Term Care Insurance* (available at www.financialratingsseries.com/page/pr_boxset). Get educated on Medicare benefits and Medicare supplement insurance. Also available is the *Consumer Guide to Medicare Supplement Insurance* (available at www.financialratingsseries.com/page/pr_boxset).

Remember, the more you know now, the easier it will be to plan for your future care. And having a good plan for your future care will allow you to more thoroughly enjoy your "Golden Years!"

Appendix

Nursing Home Checklist

Nursing Home Checklist _____

Address: _____

Phone #: _____

Where you heard about it: _____

Name of Administrator: _____

Before visiting the facility, get the answers to the following essential questions:

Does the facility <u>and</u> administrator have a current license?	Yes or No
Is the facility Medicaid certified?	Yes or No
What is the staff to resident ratio?	_____ staff members
	to
	_____ residents
What is the turnover rate for staff (i.e. What is the average length of employment?)	_____ years
How long has the management been employed at the facility?	_____ years
What is the occupancy rate?	_____
Are they admitting new residents?	Yes or No
Can the facility meet the essential special needs from your criteria list?	Yes or No
How far is the nearest hospital in case of emergencies?	_____ miles
Is the resident's personal physician able to make visits?	Yes or No
Is the location convenient for family visits?	Yes or No

While you're visiting the facility, inspect each of the following:

Safety and Cleanliness

	Ideal	- Conditions -			Poor
Quality of lighting	1	2	3	4	5
Clear hallways and cleanliness of floors	1	2	3	4	5
Handrails in hallways, bathrooms, and patient rooms	1	2	3	4	5
Emergency call buttons near the toilet	1	2	3	4	5
Sturdy chairs and tables	1	2	3	4	5
Well-marked exits that are unlocked from the inside	1	2	3	4	5
Dry floors near the entrance during inclement weather	1	2	3	4	5
General odor of the facility	1	2	3	4	5
Access for walkers/wheelchairs in hallways/dining areas	1	2	3	4	5
Cleanliness of kitchen	1	2	3	4	5
Freshness of food	1	2	3	4	5
Orderliness of trash disposal	1	2	3	4	5

How are contagious diseases handled? Does the facility have a designated isolation area for residents with contagious illnesses?

_____

_____

Quality of Care

Are most residents in their rooms with the doors closed?	Yes or No
If doors are open, do you see residents in restraints?	Yes or No
Do rooms have personal touches, such as family photos, flowers?	Yes or No
Are there extra chairs for visitors in each room?	Yes or No
Are residents allowed to choose whether they eat their meal in the dining room or in their room?	Yes or No
Does the staff use residents' names when speaking with them?	Yes or No

Are there designated areas for social and recreational activities?   Yes or No

If so, do you see the recreational areas being utilized?   Yes or No

Is a menu with choices offered at mealtime?   Yes or No

Is a licensed nutritionist in charge of meal plans?   Yes or No

Are there extra chairs for visitors in each room?   Yes or No

Are nutritious snacks available between meals?   Yes or No

How are special diets handled?

_____

_____

How often are residents bathed? _____

How often are bed linens changed? _____

	Ideal	- Conditions -		Poor
Adequate and appealing meals	1	2	3	4	5
Residents finishing their meals	1	2	3	4	5
Staff's demeanor	1	2	3	4	5
Residents' demeanor toward staff	1	2	3	4	5
Residents' demeanor toward visitors	1	2	3	4	5
Residents well-groomed with hair brushed	1	2	3	4	5
Outdoor sitting area	1	2	3	4	5

Staff Qualifications

What are the staff's qualifications (R.N., L.P.N., C.N.A.)?

_____

_____

What training is provided to new employees?

_____

_____

How is the staff supervised? (staff should be well-supervised, preferably by qualified Registered Nurses, not just one facility administrator)

_____

_____

Is there a doctor on call at all times?   Yes or No

Is there a dentist available?   Yes or No

Are volunteers utilized? What type of roles do they take in the facility ?

_____

_____

QUESTIONS FOR ADMINISTRATION

Staff Qualifications

What situation would warrant a resident's restraint? Instead of restraints, does the facility have bed alarms to warn the nursing staff a patient is trying to get out of bed?

_____

_____

How is a resident's privacy and security ensured?

_____

_____

Does the facility have a family/resident council, or similar board of external members to represent residents rights?

_____

_____

How are conflicts between patient preference and facility rules handled?

_____

_____

Do they offer recent references (less than a year old)?

_____

_____

Additional POSITIVES:

_____

_____

_____

_____

Additional NEGATIVES:

_____

_____

_____

_____